I will accept what I cannot change, but I will not accept what I can change.

I will change everything that is stopping me from getting better or doing better...because I am on the way to change.

We have constructed a wall around ourselves and we are all trapped in it. This attitude is stopping us from leading a good life and excelling in our professional lives. who is responsible for all this? is an external factor is responsible for this or I am responsible for this? what is all this? would you like to know it and change it? if your answer is yes, then you should definitely read this book. because we can change ourselves but not others.

Life@360 degree change

By Anand A. Devchakke

Mobile: 9822510641

Mail: anand_a_dev@rediffmail.com

First Published in 2022

Becomeshakespeare.com

One Point Six Technologies Pvt Ltd
123, Building J2, Shram Seva Premises,
Wadala Truck Depot,
Wadala (East), Mumbai 400037, India
T: +91 8080226699

ISBN - 978-93-5610-847-9

Dedicated with utmost respect and
love to mother Arundhati and father
Achyut Sadashiv Devchakke

About the Author

"Victory can be certain only when you do not fear to lose, otherwise both are equally likely!"

– Anand D

Anand is a leading Author, Trainer and a Great Influential Public Speaker with having long experience of 10 years in the field of Training and Development. His debut book "Life@360-degree change" is receiving a very good response from the readers and book lovers and helping more and more people to change their life with some easy changes. Anand has inspired many peoples with his speeches and writings. He has received many awards for his outstanding work and also interviewed by many prestigious media platforms.

Few of them is as follows –

1)   SAHITYA KOSH SAMMAN for 2021
2)   AUTHOR HONOUR PAPERBACK BOOK JULY 2021

3) Tagore COMMEMORATIVE Honouree 2021

4) Special Interview Coverage from Maharashtra as FABULOUS PERSONALITY –Literature Special 2021 on the platform – TBMJ

5) LITERARY ICON – 2021 on National Authors Day – 1st Nov.

6) Forever STAR INDIA Award – 2021 - FSIA

7) Nation Choice Author Award – 2021 by Glantor X

8) India Prime Author Award – 2022 By FoXclues India

9) FINALIST AUTHOR OF THE YEAR 2021 and INSPIRING AUTHOR FOR 2022 – NE8x Litfest 2021

10) Featured among "Inspiring INDIANS 2022 AWARDEE" - NE8x

11) Special 2-Page Interview coverage by online premier magzine – MyPencildotcom – Feb 2022 edition

12) **Special Interview Coverage in Leading News Paper – Hindustan Chronicles:** The Change Maker – 18th Feb 2022: Trending

Anand mainly works in the areas of: –

- Time Management and Goal Achievement with 7 keys formula

- High Impact Public Speaking and Presentation to influence the audience

- The Art of Communication and Developing the Relations

- The "4 Q" Secrets of Successful Journey …

- The Real Meaning of Spirituality and Human Life

Apart from this he also provides personalised guidence on Public Speaking, Presentation and Communication. His guidence has helped many peoples to deliver high impact speech and influence the audience. He has influenced and helped more than 7000 peoples to develop their personalities and lead the life. Because of this he is known as The Change – Maker. Being part of MCED experts panel (Maharashtra Council for Entreprenuership Development) he has helped especially new and small / medium Entrepreneurs to design and develop a business strategy/planning mainly during their start up age. Anand believes in "Get mindshare to get Market Share" and "Life gives us nothing; it just returns us for what we did"

He has done his Post Graduation in Economics from the University of Pune.

Welcome to the world of Change!!

Table of Contents

Chapter 1

My reasons behind writing this book

Hello friends,

I hope all of you are well. deep gratitude for reading about my views. I am here to talk about life in general. since many years I have been thinking, that how can we make our life easier? Or how can we enjoy a stress-free life? By stress free, I mean a life devoid of expectations, jealousy, hate and competition. All of these aspects are part of our perspective, thinking process and behavior, we carry their heavy weight all through our lives. We have developed these aspects with experience and age. I always think, that what was our behavior like, when we were kids? how we use to play without a care in the world, our lives were completely free of stress.

But, as we grow old, our responsibilities keep on increasing and the world starts expecting more, much more from us. By this time, we have created a set pattern of living for ourselves and we live our lives according to it. This unique pattern encompasses our individual thinking, specific opinion, a set pattern of talking to ourselves, a set pattern of talking with others, etc. After some years its very challenging to change these set patterns, ways and we are caught in midst of this turmoil. Maybe this is what the world calls" Generation Gap". Slowly we sink so deep in the marshland called life that we experience a strange monotony. and this monotony becomes the reason for our worry, hopelessness and anger, and this may affect our lives and might have unforeseen impact on it.

Imagine, its Sunday today and you are watching a movie on television . but you don't find the movie interesting, what will you do then? Will you change the whole tv or just the channel or the movie? What is easier? No doubt, changing the channel or the film, right? In the same way, we don't have to change our life, but change that channel of our life which is the reason of this monotony. so that we can enjoy some fresh breeze in our lives and move forward with a carefree life. A little change in our thinking, our perception, philosophy will bring a big change in our lives, these small changes will help us lead a better and more fulfilling life.

We can bring back our enthusiasm □□

We can bring back our confidence □□

We can bring back interest in our lives □□

We can bring back inspiration in our lives □□

We can bring back energy in our lives □□

Yes, we can bring back all those things, which were present in our childhood and we have lost them now. I have to ask you some questions now, please answer in yes or no .

When you wake up in the morning do you feel excited for the new day? When you go to your office, does your work inspire/ excite you?

Do you feel light and stress free the whole day long?

Is your relation with others improving? Are you happy with yourself?

Are you laughing naturally? Are you hopeful for the future? If your answer for all these question is in negative, then you are reading the right book

. today everything in life has become a formality and in this formal world we have lost our natural life . we have formed a wall of special thoughts, perspective, opinions and philosophies around us and we need to bring some changes in it. If we don't change that, we will continue living the same life which we have been leading since many years.

Change disbelief with belief.

Change hatred with love.

Respect yourself and accept yourself as you are.

Look at opportunities not problems.

With such changes you can lead a better personal and professional life. It is not necessary that all these features are applicable for you, but some may be. It is your decision. I am experiencing all these changes in my life that is why through this book I am trying to share this thought with all of you □

Whatever I have written in this book, I have picked up from many good books which I have read and from my own experience, and I have serialized all that information properly and presented before you .

Are you ready for all these changes?

Lesson 2

Change your perception towards life.

What do we perceive about life today?

What do we think about life?

How is life?

Answers to these questions will inform us about our life style. How are we living? which changes are needed to live happily? I feel that as we age, we develop a special point of view or perception towards life. This depends on our life experiences and we live our lives according to these point of views. as time passes this special point of view is strengthened. Whatever happens in our life we see it though that perception only. We do get influenced by others' opinions and reactions. in the end we are caught in this distinct circle and we start defining our life within that circle.

Some people perceive life as a struggle ....,

some people see it as a burden of stress and responsibilities, for some people life is simply boring.

Some people feel that life is a problem...

There are some people who see life as an opportunity.

Do you know that in this life there is nothing which we can call as our own? that is why we don't know that what is right and what is wrong. For some people life can be full of problems and for some it can be an opportunity. But it's a decision which you need to make for yourself.

I feel that life gives us an opportunity to choose a better way. Whatever we choose we get results according to that. If you feel that life is full of problems and stress then you need to change this perception, because there is other side of the coin also, in which we see life as full of opportunities. so, tell me, which direction would you like to choose? This change will help us to see an opportunity in every problem and this way, our lives will become easier and better.

Till now I had perceived life as problems and stress and I was sick of it.Because of this thought process I was unable to see the other side of the coin, which was full of opportunities. but now I have changed my perspective. Instead of thinking about life as problems, stress and struggle, I feel my life is an opportunity for me to make my future better. This outlook of life has made my life easier and I have reclaimed my joy of living.

Now instead of getting harassed by problems or stress I get inspired to face them and win over them. I have said goodbye to my worries and after that my life has become much better.

Whenever you are facing a problem or stress, before reacting to it, just question yourself, is there any opportunity hidden in this problem? What is science? science is nothing but an opportunity to make human life better through various challenges and problems faced by us.

Are you ready for this change?

Chapter 3

Change the way you talk to yourself

Till now we have discussed that how we should change our point of view about external problems. But we need to make some essential changes in the ways we talk to ourselves too.

Do you know that maximum time we speak to ourselves and this is responsible for developing our inherent personality? Sometimes we are aware of this, but mostly this keeps on playing in the background, and we are not aware of it. Sometimes, while talking to ourselves we use insulting or negative words. This impacts our confidence and distorts our image. Due to this we start disrespecting ourselves and become careless because we feel there is nothing more left in life. This is like a vicious cycle of negativity. This will continue and we will receive results according to that. We need to break this vicious cycle and come out of it. New world is ready to welcome you. The time has come to feel this change yourself.

There are lot of professional courses which teach us how to converse with the world, but there are no courses available which teach us, how to converse with yourself?

Our inherent way of talking to ourselves develops our personality. Especially for this reason, we need to check that while talking to ourselves we use which kind of provisions/ words and thoughts? What do we tell ourselves about others? The dialogue is positive or negative? It is optimistic or pessimistic? All this is very important because these things will trouble you a lot. You hope that others should change, but this rarely happens. Habit of talking negative things with oneself manifests into problems for you and your health. This creates problems in day-to-day life also. It reduces your inspirations and happiness. This also develops a negative circle around you and you start feeling that you are not progressing in life.

So the question arises that how will you control this tendency? Just be careful and be vigilant about the manner in which you speak to yourself. For example, if you are not happy with some system our company management, so instead of using negative words we can say that management or process has lots of scope for improvement our you hope that improvements will be implemented. This will make you feel confident and comfortable ▢ you can keep yourself away from those worries which have cropped up due to negative opinions. Hence it will not become a hindrance in your job and performance. We can also improve our relations with the help of good self-discussion. if you use good and confident words while talking to yourself, it means that you respect yourself and this will reflect in your behavior with the external world.

In the beginning, it is difficult to change, but slowly and steadily, by checking your negativity you can change your personality.

So, are you ready for this transformation?

Chapter 4

Accept some facts of life.

Nature has given us lots of freedom to develop and live our life in a particular way. this is the reason that why we can control some things and develop them according to our like and dislikes. but some things and incidence are beyond our control. If we ponder on these incidents our points, they can spoil our daily routine our can affect our life tremendously. I am sure you must have understood, what I am talking about.Instead of over thinking and analysis we should learn to accept some things as they are. This will save your energy which you can use in other productive works.

When we talk about game, we should know that game means victory or defeat. If somebody will win then somebody is bound to lose, this is part of a game. so, whenever we win, we should celebrate it, but whenever we lose, we should accept it and try for a better performance next time. If we don't accept our defeat without any legal reason, it will trouble us our we will stop improving. because of this we can lose an opportunity for our best performance. victory or defeat both are part of a game and it is important that we accept them naturally.

Many a times, we take small matters very seriously. We take lots of time to analyze a situation and get nothing in return. For this reason, we need to check everything and then decide about the next transaction.

We cannot control what others talk about us or what they think about us? But we can certainly control what we talk and what we think. We just need to accept the changes in us.

There are lots of events which take place in our life, which are a part of our life. Death is one of them. We need to accept this fact with lots of wisdom. if there is an end then there is bound to be a start, and if there is a start then there is bound to be an end. This is like a cycle and we need to accept it to live our life happily.

Most of the people amongst us remember our past and take a lot of time in remembering it. We blame ourselves for those mistakes which we did. We need to accept that we cannot go back to past and improve our mistakes.We need to think of ways of not doing such mistakes in the future

My friend was in a habit of criticizing everything. He used to spend days doing so. one day I asked him, you have been doing this thing for years, has it improved anything according to your expectations? He said there has been no change, then what have you attained by this habit? I asked him. It is important to remember that we cannot control time but we can certainly utilize time in a better way, but we need to decide and accept some facts of life so that our life becomes simpler and happier. now please feel this change within you, so are you ready for this change?

Chapter 5

Take a powerful step on the path of transformation

Since many years we have been living with a particular lifestyle. some of these life styles are not useful today. That's why we feel it is important for us to change. This is not easy but it's certainly possible.

We feel we need to take big steps to change our lives. But this cannot be true always . For example, we cannot stop thinking but we can certainly change the way we think. I am not able to do a particular thing so I should not stop that perspective. Just change the way you think. Think that anything is possible for you and your thinking is still working .

Imagine you are driving a car and you see a big pothole in the middle of the road so what will be your reaction ? Will you change the road you will steer the car in the right direction? You know the right answer .

A life is similar to steering a car. Whenever there is a problem, we should not try to change your life, we just need to steer it in the right direction . A life will progress smoothly. Whenever we are faced with challenges, we start to feel that our life has no meaning and we become sad . When we keep on living with these sad thoughts, we can lose control and our life can proceed in the wrong direction .

Now you have realized that you need to change your life , and only and only you can do it .And you take the decision to do so , but just deciding will not serve as a means to an end . You need to take a powerful step on the road of transformation . And this step will be totally different from a normal step.

A powerful step means a step taken with full confidence, which has no hidden fear our doubt in it . Whenever we decide anything we start doubting the outcome . We begin to question ourselves, we start feeling what will others think about us, what will happen? In such a way lots of doubt gives rise to lots of fear our fear stops us in taking and essential step. That's why after some efforts we come back to our old patterns, but if this is the case then how can we progress us proceed ahead

I am sure you all know that a rocket needs to have more power than earth's gravity, because earth's gravity stops the rocket from going into the sky. But once the rocket surpasses earth's gravitational force then we did not worry at all. It can fly easily, similarly for us to surpass our boundaries we need to take powerful steps. When you will surpass your boundary then everything will become easier for you. This is the reason, when in the beginning you are on the path of transformation, then you need to take powerful steps till the time you surpass your limits. When you walk, when you talk, when you think that this powerful step should reflect in all your works. walk with confidence, talk with confidence, behave with full confidence, but not with ego.

Please don't think that this is not possible now. Don't overthink. believe in yourself and start progressing on the path of change. This power will help you in surpassing your limits and will help you in enjoying every aspect of your life. That's why the promise is of a powerful step and we know that together we can do it

So, are you ready for this powerful transformation?

Chapter 6

Keep the rope of your kite tied somewhere.

Our life is filled with ups and downs. Because of this we get upset and start having a pessimistic attitude towards life. For example, a kite can fly confidently in the sky, because kite's rope is attached somewhere or is in someone's hands. Now just think, if we cut the rope of the kite, what will happen to that kite flying so confidently in the sky? The kite will lose its control and eventually will fall down.

Our life is very similar to a kite. We want to fly confidently in the open sky of our life , but if our rope is not tied anywhere, even a small gust of wind will make us lose control. That is why it is important that we should tie the rope of our life to some fixed point. It depends totally on you where you want to tie it.

When you drive a car, you face a lot of obstacles on the road. But by using the steering, accelerator and the brake in coordination you reach your destination safely. According to the need you can make changes to it .

Many people say that they don't trust anything or they try to do everything on their own. There is absolutely nothing wrong in this, but this should not be overconfidence. When you face a problem, you need to keep your hopes alive, and this work or anything that you trust, can help you in a big way. Your internal confidence should get support from your external beliefs.

And this is the reason that whenever your internal confidence weakens, your external beliefs help you, support you. External beliefs can be anything. A small inspiring thought will also help your boat in crossing the border. This belief will not let you go astray in difficult times and will help you in staying on the right course. A better coordination between your internal and external world will make you strong physically and mentally and will help you in staying happy. Are our hopes from life any different than this? Now you just need to decide a place for your belief. a place where you can tie your rope

and fly in the sky of life will full independence /
My best wishes are always with you

So,are you ready for this transformation?

Chapter 7

Your morning determines your full day

It's true that day's start determines our day. how our day will be spent, this is decided in the magical morning hours. In the morning as we open the door many external factors come inside our house. It seems they were waiting there for us since night time. Some factors can be good and some can be bad. But I know that you will let the good things stay in and will try to keep out the bad things. this is possible because of our awareness.

In the morning, when we open our eyes, we don't realize what is happening with us. Many negative thoughts enter our mind and start spreading their evil net, they stay with us and destroy the whole day. when we sleep, they wait till the morning so they can enter our thoughts. This all happens automatically and unwittingly. Would you like to know, how it happens?

Sameer is a working professional. Every day he wakes up at 6 am. In the early hours he is very energetic. Before going to the office, he switches on the television and watches the news. The news is mostly about accidents, suicides, and negative events. He watches news with a cup of tea and the negative news enters his brain and creates tension. He does not even realize this. If television is not available, he reads the newspaper. The front page is filled with negative news like accidents, war, political dramas, murders etc. At that moment he feels that the whole system is useless and there is no hope for future. Now he travels for 30-40 minutes to reach hie office, during the journey he starts surfing on his mobile and becomes active on social media, this can lead to an increase in his stress. With this stress he enters his office and waits for the day to get over. In the evening he finishes his work and returns back home. He spends some time with his family, then watches tv and then goes off to sleep. While sleeping he feels that he was not able to achieve anything great during the day, because he was pressed for time or he was not feeling up to it. The whole day he was lost in negative and scary thoughts. This happens with most of us.

Do you have any idea that how can you improve this situation? Things which are being shown on television are not in our control, but we can be selective about what we see. Social media content is not in our control, but what to read and what not to read is absolutely in our control. While going to office Sameer has two options, he can surf his mobile our he can see outside, he can see the beautiful surroundings, sunrays, fresh air, people, birds, plants, flowers and mountains. He can enjoy the scenery. These things give us a special freshness and makes us energetic and vibrant for the day ahead. If during the journey, it's not imperative to use the mobile then please enjoy your surroundings and immerse yourself in the scenery. This fills our brain with enthusiasm, allows fresh thoughts to enter our mind and increases our confidence. When you reach office with this new attitude your performance improves and you can end you day happily and satisfied. When you end your day with a sense of achievement, you will discover that your energy levels will be up even when you reach home. This energy is the secret behind many great achievements .

We live under pressure of negative thoughts and less energy and this is the reason why we don't find enough energy to start something new. This increases our stress and despondency. But it is for us to decide whether we want to waste our day or enjoy it fully, and for this purpose the most important thing is the beginning of the day .

The above lessons can be summed up in three important points

1) Avoid negative thoughts and social media in the mornings .

2) While travelling to your shop or office, enjoy the beauty of your surroundings

3) Please utilize the precious morning hours to think about yourself .

I am aware that all this is in our control and we should do it .

So, are you ready for this transformation?

Lesson 8

Be very focused on your life goals.

Just think, you are sitting in a bus and the conductor is asking you where do you want to go? Please buy a ticket. But you are still not clear about your destination, then what will happen? the conductor will ask you 3 or 4 times and then he will tell you to get down from the bus. If this is true about a normal bus ride then will it be true for our life also? Are we clear about our life goals?

On this earth, every man is lucky enough to have a wonderful life. There is no difference between rich and poor. The difference lies in our efforts, and we make efforts only when we are clear about our life goals. We can call them dedicated efforts, otherwise we will keep on fooling ourselves.

Along with being clear about our life goals we need to change our luck too. If we are clear about our life goals, we will work in that direction which will make us successful. But if we are not clear about our life goals, we will keep on fooling ourselves. we will be like some uncontrollable car. Difference between successful and unsuccessful people is only one and that is not being clear about your life goals.

If I know that I want to be singer or a cricketer or a writer then I will use all my resources to this effect and keep on working towards my goals. With my continuous efforts I will keep on improving and this improvement will help me attain a special life. One day my life will change for the better and I will attain all that I have dreamt about. I am aware that in this competitive world only success is seen as superlative. In our life so many events happen which tend to make us confused. But if you are clear about your life goals, there will be no such thing which will confuse you or trouble you. This is such a change which will help you to attain your life goals in a superlative manner.

There are two kinds of people in this world, the first one is those who flow with the time and go wherever time takes them. they don't have a specific motive in life, such people keep on changing their job or business. If they lose one job, they get a second and a third job and so on and their story keeps on progressing, just to earn a few rupees they keep on following this path and never realize their true capabilities. Later they lose all their interest and keep on following the normal path. This makes their life uninteresting. Second type of people are such people who are clear about their life goals and they are working with full focus to attain their goals. they invest all their energy on their goals and nothing can deter them or confuse them from this path.

Life is a paper full of suggestions and if you are clear about your life goals, you will receive only helpful suggestions which will help you in attaining your life goals and you will be saved from suggestions which will confuse and trouble you.

So, the question arises that how will you know about your life goals?

Recognize your passion/ likes

Everyone is precious on this Earth and has the ability to live a successful life. you need to recognize your passion and likes . Please don't be pressurized by others, many a times we select a particular job because our friend is working there, or we select a particular stream because our friend has selected that etc.But be aware, your likes or interests can be very different than your friend. you need to understand this and decide your life goals accordingly

Stop blaming others

When we are not successful, we blame our parents, teachers, friends, or the system. But have they stopped us from being successful? As I told you that everybody is born with some luck on this earth and we need to make it shine with our efforts or work. It is like Aladdin's lamp, we just need to rub it so that it shines and fulfills all our desires. People will give you lots of suggestions, it is possible that the suggestions are useful or not. But what is useful and what is not depends on your life goals. If somebody is telling you to go to left and your destination is on the right, will you be confused? that is why it is very important to remain focused and work accordingly. This is your and only your responsibility .Please accept it and if you still don't know what is your life goal, think again, recognize your life goal and start making efforts in that direction. A life without direction will confuse us and that is why it is imperative to proceed in the right direction

So, are you ready for this transformation?

43

Chapter 9

When life touches the great depths of the ocean...

Life is like an ocean, sometimes we swim on the surface and sometimes we touch the great depths of the ocean . this is the time when we think that everything is finished now . we can't see a way forward. but we tend to forget that now we have no option but to return to the surface and the journey of our success starts from this very moment. Now is the time to embark on this new journey with energy and strength.

When I read life stories of many successful people, I came to know that they have all gone through this bad phase in life. Their financial condition was bad, their relations were strained, they had lost their jobs, they were depressed and had no idea how they will move forward. But they never lost hope and found their true way in such dark times also.

If you are also facing the same situation in your life, please don't worry, because very soon you will reach the surface. After touching the lowest point there is no other option but to move upwards, it's the law of the nature

If you have not touched that depth and your life is hanging in middle, please try to move in the upward direction. if this is not possible then please go towards the lowest point and start afresh. Your decision depends on your thoughts and views about the ups and downs of life.

Never lose hope, keep it alive because time has come to reach the surface. with a few changes and efforts, you can reach the surface. Your changed perspective, notions, way of talking to yourself, powerful steps, confidence etc., all will help you reach that target point

This is the time of change, experience new changes with age old styles. because this is life undergoing a 360 degree change .